# Amazon Fever

by Kathleen Weidner Zoehfeld
illustrated by Paulette Bogan

JACKSON COUNTY LIBRARY SERVICES
MEDFORD OREGON 97501

For Ernestina
K.W.Z.


To Michael and Alyssa
P.B.


Special thanks to Jenny Lando, Science Educator,
the American Museum of Natural History.

*Library of Congress Cataloging-in-Publication Data*
Zoehfeld, Kathleen Weidner.
Amazon fever / by Kathleen Weidner Zoehfeld ; illustrated by Paulette Bogan.
    p.    cm. — (Road to reading.  Mile 4)
Summary: When Jeff accompanies his uncle to the Amazon Rain Forest to
acquire butterflies for an exhibit at the museum where his uncle works, Jeff
hopes to see real jaguars as well.
ISBN 0-307-26407-6 (pbk) — ISBN 0-307-46407-5 (GB)
[1. Butterflies—Fiction.  2. Rain forests—Amazon River Region—Fiction.
3. Brazil—Fiction.]  I. Bogan, Paulette, ill.  II. Title.  III. Series.

PZ7.Z715 Am 2001
[Fic]—dc21                                                    00-061005

**A GOLDEN BOOK • New York**
Golden Books Publishing Company, Inc. New York, New York 10106

ISBN: 0-307-26407-6 (pbk)
ISBN: 0-307-46407-5 (GB)

10   9   8   7   6   5   4   3   2   1

# Contents

## 1 / El Tigre

The jaguar's yellow eyes gleamed through the dark jungle leaves. His lips pulled up in a snarl. His sharp teeth flashed in the dim light. The three-hundred-pound cat crouched on a branch. He was about to leap!

I love looking at the jaguar at the Wye Museum. Uncle Roy calls him

*El Tigre*. That's Spanish for jaguar. Too bad *El Tigre* is stuffed and stuck in a display case.

"I'd like to see a jaguar for real. Right up close," I told Uncle Roy.

Uncle Roy didn't answer. He was bringing palm trees and other tropical plants into the new greenhouse.

Uncle Roy runs this museum. It was his idea to add a greenhouse to the Amazon Rain Forest exhibit. That way, he said, visitors can feel what it's like to walk in the jungle.

It's a cool idea. Still, I don't think it will be as great as the jungle-cat part.

After all, the greenhouse will only have flowers and bugs and stuff.

"Why can't we get a live jaguar?" I asked Uncle Roy.

He looked at me from behind a potted fern. "Jeff, this is a natural history museum," he said, "not a zoo!"

"But we're going to have live *butterflies*," I argued.

He gave me another look.

"Okay, okay. I guess there's not much danger a butterfly will eat a visitor," I admitted.

Uncle Roy smiled. "That's the good thing about butterflies."

I stared at the old butterfly display case. It had been in the museum for the last century or so. The case went from the floor to the ceiling. Behind the glass, hundreds of butterflies were pinned in rows.

"They're pretty," I said. "Pretty boring, that is." I laughed at my joke. Uncle Roy didn't.

"Well, then you'd better not come to Brazil with me next week," he said.

"Not come?" I cried. "Are you kidding?" I had already been to the Sahara Desert with him, looking for dinosaur fossils. Now he was planning a trip to the Amazon Rain Forest.

"Jeff, the whole point of the trip is to get butterflies," Uncle Roy warned.

"If *you* want to chase butterflies, that's fine," I told him. "*I'll* be on the trail of the wild jaguar!"

Uncle Roy smiled and shook his head. Maybe he didn't believe I'd find a jaguar. But I was going to try!

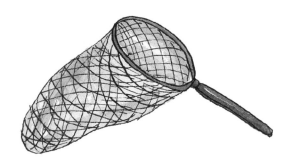

## 2 / Down on the Farm

Three days later, Uncle Roy and I landed in Manaus. A blast of muggy heat hit me as I stepped off the plane.

"Is it always this hot?" I asked.

"This hot and hotter," said Uncle Roy.

Manaus is in Brazil's Amazon Rain Forest. A city smack in the middle of the jungle seemed weird to me, but Uncle Roy said it's an important port. From here, stuff like rubber and lumber is shipped down the Amazon River to the bigger cities on the coast.

Uncle Roy rented a jeep and we drove north. In lots of places, the forest had been cleared away for houses and farms, but in some spots, the trees crowded right up to the road. I peered into the deep, dark jungle. I couldn't wait to get in there.

"Here we are!" cried Uncle Roy. The jeep bumped down a muddy driveway. A small house and some low buildings stood in a clearing.

"Uh, Uncle Roy? This isn't the jungle," I pointed out. "It's a farm."

"Right!" declared Uncle Roy. "A butterfly farm."

"A butterfly FARM?" I cried. "I thought we were hunting butterflies in the jungle."

"Patience, Jeff. The scientists at the farm collect different types of butterflies in the jungle. From the few they take, they raise hundreds," he said. "We'll order all the pupae we need from the farm."

"So we're going to spend the whole

day looking at little bug eggs?" I was already hot and miserable. Now I was going to be bored, too.

"Not eggs. Pupae," corrected Uncle Roy. "First a caterpillar hatches out of an egg. In a few weeks, the caterpillar attaches itself to a twig and forms a hard shell around itself. That's the pupa."

"I know, I know," I said. "And after a few more weeks, the adult butterfly comes out of the pupa. I was kidding about the bug eggs. We learned about metamorphosis at school this year."

"A fascinating process!" Uncle Roy declared. He and one of the butterfly farmers began going over a list.

Under my breath I grumbled, "At this rate, I'll *never* find a jaguar."

Uncle Roy peered up at me from his list. "Butterflies, Jeff. We're here for butterflies."

# 3 / The Jungle at Last!

The next morning, some of the
scientists from the farm were getting
ready for a research trip. They were
heading into the jungle!

"Can we go with them?" I asked.

"I don't know," Uncle Roy said.
"The jungle's a wild place. Do you
think you're ready for it?"

He had to be joking! "Let me at it!" I cried.

Uncle Roy laughed. No way he was going to pass up a trip like this!

I helped the scientists pack food, camping gear, and the special butterfly traps. They said we would be studying the areas where butterflies lived. We'd also collect new butterflies for the farm.

"If we're lucky," said Uncle Roy, "we might even see a ghostwing butterfly."

A *ghost* butterfly? Maybe there was more to this butterfly hunting than I thought.

# FIELD JOURNAL—DAY 1

We drove for most of the day. Then we set up camp at the edge of the forest.

Suddenly, it was raining buckets! We dashed into our tents. Uncle Roy put our camera in a plastic bag to keep it dry. As if anything here could ever stay dry! Guess that's why they call it a rain forest.

When the rain stopped, the air was hotter and stickier than ever. The ground was mucky.

Now it's evening. Boinging, scritchy-scratching, whirring, hooting, thumping sounds are coming from the forest. Uncle Roy says it's bugs and tree frogs. But how can little bugs and frogs make such HUGE weird noises? They must be monsters!

No way I'm EVER going out there!

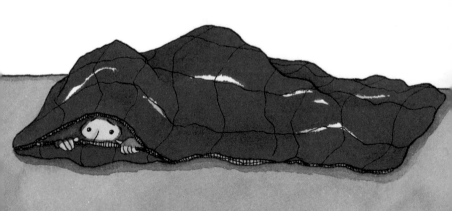

"Up and at 'em!" Uncle Roy shouted early the next morning.

I remembered the monster noises from last night and sank deeper into my sleeping bag. "You'd better go on without me!" I shouted.

High in the treetops, the parrots were squeaking and the scarlet macaws were squawking.

Uncle Roy unzipped the tent door and motioned me out. Nervously, I went to help pack up our tents. This was it. We were going in there. Into the jungle! It's what I had wanted all along. Now I wasn't so sure.

I watched a lizard amble out on a branch to enjoy the morning sun. He seemed friendly enough. Suddenly, I heard a deep, howling roar!

*Jaguar!* I thought. I dove into one of the parked jeeps.

"Just listen to the howler monkeys!" Uncle Roy said to the other scientists.

I crept out of the jeep, hoping he hadn't noticed. He looked me over. "Something wrong?"

"I'm fine," I said, slipping on my backpack. "Nice monkeys."

We started back down the trail. A small tea-colored river was to our left. The dark-green forest was on our right.

Uncle Roy handed me a butterfly net.

"No, thanks," I said, waving the wimpy-looking thing away. "That will be no help with jaguars." I tried to look brave.

"Now Jeff," said Uncle Roy, "I don't know about seeing any jaguars, but I do want you to be careful today. Remember—always look before you put your hands or feet down. The jungle is full of— Oh my gosh!"

He stopped so suddenly, I almost crashed into him.

"What?" I cried. I was afraid to look.

He pointed to a wide muddy patch on the riverbank. It was covered with hundreds of yellow-green butterflies. "Pierids feeding in the mud!" Uncle Roy shouted.

"Mmm, tasty," I said.

We stopped and watched them for a long time. The scientists took lots of notes and collected a few butterflies. Later, they found some pierid pupae attached to leaves.

"How do you know these things are pupae?" I asked. "They look like bird poop!"

"They look like that so birds and other enemies won't eat them," Uncle Roy explained.

"Ew, good idea," I said. I guess these butterflies were not so dumb after all.

# FIELD JOURNAL—DAY 2, MORNING

○     While everyone was busy watching butterflies, I watched for danger. First I spotted what looked like an alligator, floating in the river. Uncle Roy said it was a caiman.

○     Then there were the snakes. A giant anaconda can swallow a caiman in one gulp. Uncle Roy says anacondas don't eat people. (Right.)

○     He warned me AGAIN always to look where I put my feet.

Some types of poisonous snakes like to hide in the leaves on the ground or under fallen logs.

And did I mention the bugs?

I was watching out for snakes when a hairy tarantula strolled right past my feet! I have never seen such a big spider. He IS a monster!

Still no jaguars.

MONSTER SPIDER →

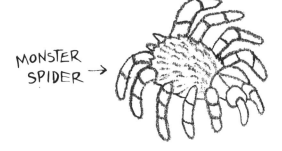

# 4 / Ghost Butterflies

After a late-morning snack, we got back on the trail into the forest.

"Look!" Uncle Roy cried. He pointed one way, then another. Butterflies were everywhere!

We spotted glimmering blue morpho butterflies bobbing up and down in the sunlight. They looked like

pieces of sky that had come loose.

The owl butterflies were harder to find. They stood perfectly still on the vines. The big fake eyes on their wings seemed to stare at us.

Tiger-striped butterflies zipped and zoomed across our path.

Each time we saw a different type of butterfly, the scientists stopped to take notes.

Butterflies weren't the only bugs out. The air was thick and still. The mosquitoes were making me itch. I swatted at them with a leaf as we pushed deeper into the jungle.

Then I saw a butterfly with wings as clear as glass. It fluttered slowly in the dark leaves and disappeared. Like a ghost!

"Hey, Uncle Roy," I called, "I think I just saw a ghostwing!"

Uncle Roy came over. "If you did, maybe we can lure it into a trap."

We found a little clearing near a stream and put up our tents. Then we carried the traps to a special place in the forest. The scientists showed me how to set up the nets. We used rotten bananas for bait.

"Whew, this stinks! Butterflies actually like this stuff?" I asked.

Still, it wasn't as bad as the bait I found Uncle Roy collecting—bird poop. REAL bird poop!

"Ghostwings love it," he said cheerfully.

"I can't believe the weird things butterflies eat!" I cried.

Once the traps were ready, the
grown-ups fixed *our* dinner in the
screened-in dining tent. We settled in
to camp for the night.

Fried banana mush for
supper. Oh, yum. If I eat
enough of that stuff, I'll turn
into butterfly bait myself!

After dinner we had to move
our tents. Army ants invaded
our camp. Millions of them! I
tried to stomp them, but they
bit at my legs like crazy. Uncle

Roy says the only thing to do
with army ants is to get out of
their way.

I just hope I got all the ants
out of my sleeping bag!

More hoots, clicks, screaks,
and thumps out there tonight. I
think I'm getting used to this.

# 5 / Lost in the Jungle

The next morning, Uncle Roy couldn't wait to see what we'd caught in our traps.

He pulled on one boot. "Ouch, ouch, ouch!" he cried. He yanked it off and dropped it.

Uncle Roy needs to listen to his own rules. Like the one about always

watching where you put your feet.

A scorpion crawled out of his boot.
It looked more annoyed than Uncle
Roy. "Wow," I said. "I didn't know they
had those in the jungle, too."

"Apparently so," he growled,
holding his stung foot in his hands.

One of the scientists brought over the first-aid kit. "Is he going to be okay?" I asked.

She told me that most scorpion bites were no worse than a bad bee sting. Still, Uncle Roy would have to be grounded in his tent all morning, just to be sure.

"I'll be fine," Uncle Roy grumbled. He propped up his foot and started writing in his journal. He looked pretty mad if you ask me.

"I'll check the traps for you," I volunteered.

"Unh," grunted Uncle Roy. He

didn't even look up from his journal. I grabbed the net he'd tried to give me the day before. Maybe I could catch some cool butterfly to cheer him up.

Near the traps I found a fallen log where I could sit. There were plenty of butterflies in the traps already, and at least one ghostwing!

As I sat scribbling notes, I saw a dark butterfly with red and yellow spots flitting past. *I bet Uncle Roy would like that one!* I thought.

"Never go into the jungle alone," I heard his voice in my head warning me. So, I hardly went far at all.

The butterfly landed on a leaf. I
swooped my net toward it, but it flew
off. I pushed through some bushes
and tried again. It dipped in and out
between some branches and settled on
a flower. I swung my net.

"Gotcha!" I cried. I looked in. Empty.

Disappointed, I turned back toward camp. "Butterfly hunting's harder than I thought," I mumbled.

But the jungle had closed in around me. Where was the camp? All I could see were leaves and more leaves! I stumbled forward. I forgot to watch where I put my feet. Something slithered just inches from my toes. I began to sweat.

"Help," I croaked. I was lost. Lost in the Amazon jungle!

I heard footsteps rustling in the bushes nearby. JAGUAR! I squeezed against a tree and held my breath.

The bushes parted. It was Uncle Roy! He hobbled into the clearing. "Jeff, how many times have I told you not to—" He stopped in mid-sentence and stared at the top of my head.

"Good heavens!" he gasped. "It's a *Heliconius nattereri.*"

"A what?" I cried. What was a Helen-a-whatsis? A snake? Hanging over my head? I didn't dare move a muscle.

The other scientists pressed through the bushes. They stared at me, too.

"It's amazing."

"It must like the scent of Jeff's shampoo."

"Haven't seen one of those here in years." The scientists spoke in hushed voices.

"What? What?" I cried. I had no idea what they were talking about.

"Congratulations, Jeff. You found a very rare longwing butterfly," Uncle Roy said.

"Really?" I breathed again. "Not a snake?"

Uncle Roy focused the camera on the butterfly in my hair. I stood as still as I could while he took pictures. Then the butterfly flew off in a dark flash of yellow and red.

"That's the one I was after!" I cried. "She's neat, but what's the big deal?"

"This area has been recovering from overfarming and lumbering for years," Uncle Roy explained. "To see this butterfly back means that its home is getting healthy again."

"Guess you're healthy again, too." I pointed at Uncle Roy's foot.

He grinned. "I'm getting there. Besides, it was boring sitting in the tent."

I patted him on the back. "Patience, Uncle Roy."

# 6 / Butterflies at the Wye

A week later, we were back at the Wye Museum. Uncle Roy had one of the photos of me and little "Helen" blown up and framed. He hung it in the Amazon Rain Forest exhibit.

The pupae the farmers had packed and shipped for us had begun to hatch. Already the new greenhouse was filled

with butterflies. And visitors!

"Hey, he's the one in the picture!"
I heard a little boy shout. He was
pointing to me.

"Isn't it great to be famous?" Uncle
Roy remarked.

I laughed, but I didn't exactly *feel*
famous. "Uh, Uncle Roy, you probably

didn't notice, but I was just a little scared out there in the jungle."

"You seemed brave enough to me, Jeff," he said. "Besides, it's always smart to be a little afraid of animals as powerful as jaguars."

"And scorpions?"

"Them, too."

"I still wish I'd seen a jaguar while I was there—just not right up close."

"I know," said Uncle Roy. "But jaguars are getting scarce. They need a lot of rain forest to live in. So much of the jungle is gone now. Most of the jaguars that are left have been forced into more remote areas."

"The same way the little Helen butterflies were forced out of their home?" I asked.

"Pretty much," said Uncle Roy.

We noticed a bunch of kids staring at a ghostwing. It had landed on a girl's shoulder.

"One of their favorite foods is bird poop," I explained. I think the kids were impressed.

"Do you think we'll be able to have a few Helen butterflies here someday, too?" I asked Uncle Roy. "Live ones, I mean. Not just pictures."

"Mmm... it *would* be amazing to have some here, wouldn't it?"

I could tell what was on his mind. "Guess we'll have to go back soon and see how they're doing," I suggested. "The Helens *and* the jaguars."

"Exactly what I was thinking," said Uncle Roy.

"I knew it!" I cried.

We walked down the halls of the Wye Museum, past mummies and swords and ancient jewels.

"But, in the meantime," said Uncle Roy, "we've got a few other exhibits that need new treasures, don't you think?"